CERAMIC TILE
ESSENTIALS

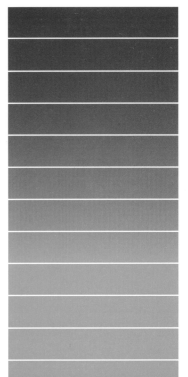

COWLES
Creative Publishing, Inc.

Minnetonka, Minnesota, USA

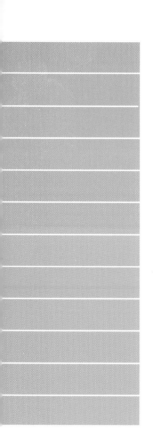

Credits

Copyright © 1997
Cowles Creative Publishing, Inc.
Formerly Cy DeCosse Incorporated
5900 Green Oak Drive
Minnetonka, Minnesota 55343
1-800-328-3895
All rights reserved
Printed in U.S.A.

COWLES
Creative Publishing, Inc.
Minnetonka, Minnesota, USA

President/COO: Iain Macfarlane
Executive V.P.: William B. Jones
Group Director, Book Development: Zoe Graul

Created by: The Editors of Cowles Creative Publishing, Inc.,
in cooperation with Black & Decker.  is
a trademark of the Black & Decker Corporation and is
used under license.

Cover Photo Courtesy of: Trade Commission of Spain

Printed on American paper by:
Quebecor Printing
00 99 98 97 / 5 4 3 2 1

Books available in this series:

Wiring Essentials
Plumbing Essentials
Carpentry Essentials
Painting Essentials
Flooring Essentials
Landscape Essentials
Masonry Essentials
Door & Window Essentials
Roof & Siding Essentials
Deck Essentials
Porch & Patio Essentials
Built-In Essentials

Contents

Choosing The Right Tile

Because the selection of tile types is so diverse, you can find ceramic and natural tile that is appropriate for almost any application imaginable. The key is selecting the right tile for the right job. Whether you're choosing tile for a shower area, a countertop or an entryway, there will be plenty of options for the type of ceramic tile that fits your lifestyle needs.

Ceramic and natural tiles can be used in new construction or renovations. They make durable and decorative surfaces for floors, walls, countertops, tables, fireplaces, stairways and ceilings. You can use tile to cover surfaces that are straight or curved, cornered or angular. There's hardly an interior setting where ceramic or natural tile couldn't be used. Outside the house, ceramic and natural tile are excellent choices for patios, pool surrounds and hot tub areas, fountains and water gardens.

Because of its formal appeal and historic ties to royalty and places of worship, many people consider ceramic tile a luxury, when in reality it is a very affordable option. For example, the cost of material for a ceramic floor is about the same as a vinyl floor. The installation cost will be more expensive for ceramic tile, but it will last much longer, spreading the cost out over a longer period of time and in the long run be more cost effective. Tiling a wall or countertop will be more costly initially than painting, hanging wallpaper or installing plastic laminate, but the tile will still look good when the other materials are faded and worn and ready to be replaced. And because ceramic and natural tiles are more resistant to water than other materials, they are more practical for almost all residential applications.

Grout is used to support and protect the edges of the tile, not to affix it to the subsurface. Although it is not considered part of the design process, selecting the proper grout can make a dramatic difference in the look and performance of a ceramic tile application. There is a wide selection of grout colors to choose from. There are basically two types of grout; cement-based and epoxy grouts. Cement-based grouts are cheaper and are water-resistant, but not absolutely waterproof.

Epoxy grouts are highly waterproof and resistant to most stains. Each type has varying performance characteristics; the type you choose will depend on the design scheme and level of use.

Ceramic and natural stone walls, floors and countertops are easy to care for, especially when stain-resistant grout is used. Tile floors should be swept or vacuumed on a regular basis to remove gritty particles that may cause scratching. Ceramic floors can be cleaned by wiping them with a damp mop or sponge. Even when they are neglected for a long time, the lustrous sheen can usually be brought back with a good washing.

Tile is also easy to replace if needed. When wall-to-wall carpeting gets a burn, you usually have to replace the entire piece. However, if damage occurs to a tiled floor, cracked or loose tiles and damaged grout can easily be repaired without tearing out the entire installation. If you want to make changes for aesthetic reasons, most tile installations can be restyled, accented or added to without removing all of the existing tile.

The warm tones and rough texture *of these Italian ceramic tiles gives them an old-world look. A mosaic-style design uses pieces of the same earth-tone tiles, giving the setting a rich, refined appearance.*

Ceramic tile has more practical applications and natural elegance than almost any surface material imaginable. An array of ceramic tiles is combined to create a relaxed, contemporary interior that has a casual elegance and is also practical and easy to care for. Stylish ceramic tiles protect the countertop and add a polished sophistication to the area surrounding this wet bar.

New sealants and waxes *can add labor-saving finishes to tiles used in areas that get extra hard wear, such as entryways and hallways.*

Photo courtesy of Florida Tile Industries, Inc.; Rubble Tile

Choosing the right tile

Floor Tiles

Ceramic and natural tiles are strong, colorfast, water-resistant and easy to clean. They are a natural choice for floor surfaces. Ceramic floor tiles are thicker and more durable than wall tiles because they need to be able to handle heavy traffic in wet entryways, and drips and spills in kitchens and bathrooms.

The first thing to consider when choosing a floor tile is how much exposure to moisture the surface will get. Next, determine the amount of foot traffic and wear the surface will have to endure. Ceramic floor tiles should have either a glazed, or partially glazed surface. Unglazed tiles are not as water-resistant or as dense. Glazed tiles have a ceramic coating fired onto them at high temperatures, which makes them stronger.

When selecting glazed floor tiles it is important to choose a tile with a glaze that is appropriate for the location and level of wear it will need to withstand. Glazed floor tiles are rated by the manufacturer according to resistance to wear in various applications. Look for tiles whose wear rating matches the needs of the floor you are going to tile. Although tile is very hard and durable, some areas, such as kitchen countertops, where chopping of hard objects occurs, have a higher risk of breakage.

Tile is classified as light traffic, medium traffic, heavy traffic and commercial. "Light traffic" tile is for areas that are walked on with soft footwear or bare feet. Because they don't need to tolerate as much wear, light traffic tiles don't need to be as strong or as durable as tiles in other applications. "Medium traffic" tile is able to handle normal footwear and has a medium resistance to scratching. This is not a tile for heavy traffic areas, where dirt and grit are dragged in from outside. "Heavy traffic" tile is acceptable for most residential and light commercial applications. This is the rating you should look for when choosing tile for entryways, kitchens, balconies and terraces, as well as a number of other areas, both indoors and out. "Commercial" tiles are also suitable for many residential applications.

The uniform shape and small size *of these floor tiles creates a pattern that pulls the space together. The simplicity of the pattern keeps the look clean and simple.*

The rough and rustic look *of the massive stone walls and ceiling is beautifully balanced by smooth stone floor tiles. A marbled white border adds an elegant accent and frames this unusual, but very captivating, combination.*

Hard-wearing ceramic floor tiles *are a long-lasting option for busy places like playrooms. And if anyone gets a bit creative with a crayon, ceramic tiles are also easy to clean.*

A colorful and creative use of ceramic tile creates a fashionable and functional floor. A dynamic pattern combines rich colors and textures to create the look of an elegant area rug and denotes the central activity area of this kitchen.

Floor Tiles

Another important factor to consider when choosing floor tiles is the level of slip resistance that is needed. Two things affect the degree of slip resistance required: the amount of water and environmental factors. The greater chance your floor has of being exposed to water or household spills, the greater the need for slip-resistant tiles. Your need for slip-resistant tiles will also be determined by your family's lifestyle needs. For example, floors that will be used by small children, people who are physically challenged or the elderly require floor tiles with definite slip-resistant characteristics.

Floor tiles in an entryway require a surface that won't be slippery when wet, whether they are glazed or unglazed. Use glazed floor tiles with a matte finish for the areas around a shower or tub, and make sure the tile is textured for slip resistance. A tile with a glossy finish has more tendency to be slippery when wet.

Steps and stairways are other surfaces where a ceramic tile application can become one of the most dramatic elements in your home. For applications on steps and stairs it is important to take safety into account. For the treads of a stairway, select sturdy floor tiles with a textured surface. Use trim pieces to define the edges of the steps, or trim the edges with wood. With accented risers, each step is clearly defined and much safer. Install tiles across the full width of the riser, or set individual tiles as a riser accent.

Ceramic tile floors are long-lasting and easy to clean. They can also be hard and cold underfoot. Strategically placed rugs, in front of sinks and work counters, soften the look of the hard surface and minimize the impact of the cold tile.

(inset photo above) **Uniquely shaped floor and mosaic tiles** *are combined in a colorful and creative design that becomes the centerpiece of this room.*

(left) **The rich colors and precise patterns** *that comprise this polished ceramic floor design add warmth and animation to its elegant appeal.*

Floor Tiles

Climate conditions must be considered when choosing a floor tile that will have an outdoor application. Installing tile outdoors requires a tile that is frost-resistant. If you live in a climate where the ground freezes, select a type of tile that can withstand extreme changes in temperature.

Tiles for outdoor use should be textured and slip-resistant. Glazed ceramic, cut stone, terra-cotta and mosaic tiles are some of the high-quality, long-wearing tiles that bring the natural beauty of tile to an outdoor setting.

When installing patio tiles, remember to slope the site so the paved areas will drain quickly and puddles won't form.

Photo courtesy of Crossville Ceramics

The colorful mosaic tile design in this floor adds a dynamic accent to the small space. The combination of colors and shapes gives the mosaic design the illusion of being three-dimensional.

Photo courtesy of Crossville Ceramics

Not just a protective floor surface, polished ceramic creates an entryway that is pure elegance. The gleaming, high-gloss tile used in the entryway extends this protective surface into the kitchen as well.

Photo courtesy of Sicis, Rex, Gabbianelli, Bardelli, Mayo De Lucci, Italian Trade Commission - Tile Center in New York

The uneven coloring of the marble floor tiles creates a textured effect within the bands of color. Crisp white ceramic tile is used to create a contrast and set off the subtle marbling in the muted earth-tone colors of the tiles.

A clean, open atmosphere *is created by the classic pattern of the floor tile in this kitchen. The small diamond insets add a subtle element of design that works with the grid created by the large grout lines.*

The delicate marbleized veining and high-gloss finish of ceramic tile add richness to the room and provide a practical and protective surface. Rectangular wall tiles feature a decaled border that runs throughout the room and defines the top of the dado; the smaller wall tiles visually draw the space together and keep the expansive room from seeming too large. The water-resistant ceramic tiles protect the walls from damaging water and steam.

Choosing the right tile

Wall Tiles

Any wall that gets wet from being splashed or sprayed will benefit from a ceramic or natural tile surface. But don't limit ceramic tile applications strictly to these "wet surfaces." Ceramic tile can be used around doors and windows to add an artistic touch, or an interesting design element. Wall tiles are especially valuable when used to protect the bottom section of the wall, just below the chair rail. This area, sometimes called a dado, is usually located about the same height as the back of a dining chair. The dado area is often covered with ceramic tile to help protect the wall from rain-soaked clothes or muddy boots, as well as markings from chairs, tables, etc. Individual tiles can be used as accents within a larger design. Around tubs and showers, a tiled wall not only provides a decorative surface, but also one that is water-resistant, longer wearing and easier to clean.

Wall tiles are usually glazed and offer a wide variety of colors and designs. They are usually lighter and thinner than floor tiles, which makes an application on a vertical surface easier. The glaze ensures a water-resistant surface. For maximum water-resistance, use epoxy grout with wall tiles. Not only is this type of grout highly waterproof, it is also highly resistant to most stains.

A colorful geometric pattern, made of bold, bright ceramic tiles, accentuates the unique shape of this shower. The ceramic tile provides a water-resistant surface for this stylish shower surround.

This elegant tiled entryway *uses colors, textures and patterns to create a look that is simple and sophisticated. Off-white wall tiles set in a diagonal pattern and the use of larger wall tiles below the dado line help expand the sense of space in this small setting. The ceramic tile helps protect wall and floor surfaces from moisture and dirt that is dragged into this fashionable foyer.*

13

Wall Tiles

Ceramic tile is a long-wearing, waterproof surface that is also very attractive and easy to clean. Because wall tile is mounted on the wall, away from heavy traffic, the durability of the surface is not of as much importance. This means that for many wall applications, the selection of ceramic tiles that make effective wall tiles is even broader than when selecting floor tiles.

Wall tiles will often need to be finished around the edges with some kind of border or trim. Many manufacturers of wall tiles have specially shaped, matching border and trim pieces available. Border tiles are special tiles specifically shaped to finish off edges, form coves, and turn corners. There are a variety of different border tiles that

can be used to finish a wall tile application. Cove tiles are curved at the bottom and are used along the bottom row of wall tile which adjoins the floor tile to create a smooth transition. There are trim pieces for sink corners, inside and outside wall corners and bullnose tile, which is used at the edge of a wall or top of a dado. Many wall tile manufacturers now offer decorative trim pieces to coordinate with their tile selections.

Creating wall and floor tile installations that match and are properly aligned can be very tricky. Many manufacturers offer predesigned packages that include floor and wall tiles and eliminate much of the guesswork involved in coordinating the two applications.

(above) **Large wall tiles** *were used in this application to help balance and support the grand size and stature of the other architectural elements in the setting.*

(right) **Wall tiles, with the look of polished marble,** *provide an easy-to-clean, water-resistant surface.*

The coolness of polished marble finishes this room with long-lasting elegance from floor to ceiling. Finely detailed relief tiles enhance the sense of sophistication and gracefully divide the space so it is visually balanced.

A border of decorated wall tiles *frames the display shelves. The two-color design is repeated again on the back wall of the recessed shelves, which creates an interesting visual effect.*

Delicately detailed *trim and accent tiles add an elegant, subtle touch. Narrow, decorative accent tiles define the top of the dado on this wall, and visually divide the expanse of ceramic tiles.*

Seashells by the seashore *is the theme of this clever design scheme. Decorative border tiles coordinate with larger decorative wall tiles. The design pattern along the border tiles has been spot-glazed to add visual highlights and an interesting element of texture.*

16

Wall Tiles

Ceramic wall tiles are an effective choice for use on deeply set windows where the ledges act as shelves for plants or other collectibles. Ceramic tiles also make an excellent choice for use around greenhouse windows. They absorb and reflect heat to the plants, and offer easy cleanup for water and dirt spills.

Photo courtesy of Marca Corona, Italian Trade Commission - Tile Center in New York

The classic charm of old-world Italy *is re-created in this bathroom using ceramic wall tiles with a marbleized finish. The vintage appeal of the tile and its protective and long-lasting qualities make this creation a true masterpiece.*

Photo courtesy of Trade Commission of Spain

Large rectangular wall tiles *expand the sense of space in this contemporary kitchen. The geometric shapes and subtle colors in the borders give the area visual boundaries and continuity.*

The bold colors of this fire-resistant, ceramic facing contribute to the strong Southwestern influence in the styling of this room.

Photo courtesy of Heat-N-Glow Fireplace Products, Inc.

Choosing the right tile

Wall Tiles

Because of their fire-resistant qualities, many types of ceramic tile are well suited to decorating different parts of a fireplace. The hearth can be given an attractive tile surface that is also a decorative part of a room's design. An ordinary mantel can be transformed into a focal point by finishing it with an artfully designed ceramic surface. A tiled mantel creates an interesting stage for various displays. The facing, or the area surrounding the opening in a fireplace, lends itself to many creative tile opportunities. Decorative tiles that complement and enhance the rest of the design can also be applied to the front of the chimney.

Photo courtesy of Motawi Tileworks, Ann Arbor, MI; Tile Heritage Foundation

Softly textured relief tiles are used to establish the design motif of this fireplace facing. Because the decorative tiles are the same color as the background tiles, the design element is subtle.

Fire-resistant ceramic tiles *were used to form the attractive Art Deco design on the facing and the floor, in front of this fireplace. The sophisticated look of this setting is a perfect example of how a ceramic tile application can be both fun and functional.*

Large ceramic floor and wall tiles *are used to create a fire-resistant hearth and cover the front facing surface of this fireplace.*

Ceramic tiles, designed to look like naturally aged stone, *are combined with a rich wood frame to create this sleek and stylish fireplace. The fire-resistant qualities of the ceramic and marble facing also make this fireplace safe and more functional.*

Decoratively painted tiles *are used to create a vintage Victorian look for this fireplace. Plain tan tiles create the background for the decorative tiles on the facing, while black tiles make a fire-resistant surface on the floor in front of the fireplace.*

Countertop Tiles

Ceramic tile makes an excellent material for finishing almost any surface in a bathroom or kitchen. In the kitchen, ceramic tile is highly effective around the sink and stove top. The hard, durable surface won't be affected by a sharp knife or a hot pan, and grease and food stains wipe off easily.

Although ceramic tile is a very durable material, it is still susceptible to chipping or cracking if heavy items are dropped on it, or a very hot or very cold object is placed directly on top of it for a long period of time.

The physical characteristics of counter tiles are very similar to those of wall tiles. Like wall tiles, countertop tiles are available in an almost endless array of colors, shapes and sizes. They are glazed with a semigloss or high-gloss finish that maintains color intensity and makes them easy to clean.

Photo courtesy of WALKER ZANGER

Ceramic tiles are a wonderful way *to put a waterproof surface around a wet area, such as the sink in a bathroom. This ceramic tile application also incorporates ceramic tiles as a design element in a border around the sink and in various configurations on the walls and floor.*

A shiny, clean *ceramic tile surface gives this colorful countertop a special gleam. A collection of decorated tiles adds water-resistant protection to the wall behind the sink. The cheery design and sparkling appeal of the porcelain tile on the countertop and backsplash creates a setting that's bright and upbeat.*

(above) **A traditional checkerboard pattern** is given an upscaled elegance with a border of thinner tiles that liven up this classic pattern. The busy countertop pattern is balanced by a simpler, less active floor tile pattern.

(inset) **Clean, white ceramic countertops** are an excellent option in any kitchen. Here, the simple white countertops are a calm contrast to the lively tile application on these kitchen cabinets.

Countertop Tiles

Ceramic countertop tiles can be used to create a custom look. You can define the area behind the cooktop, the backsplash behind the sink or designate a workspace on a countertop.

Ceramic countertop tiles are designed primarily for use on kitchen, bathroom and other similar types of countertops. They also make a decorative and durable surface for shelves, windowsills and tabletops. They are also an easy way to add a colorful accent to a design scheme.

As with wall tiles, there are specially shaped trim tiles for countertops, which makes installation around edges, sinks, backsplashes and corners easier.

The versatility of ceramic tile allows you to create your own countertop design for a truly personalized look. The fine detail that can be accomplished with ceramic tiles is one benefit that makes this material really stand out. The more creative you can be with your installation, the more original and personalized your room will be.

Photo courtesy of Monarch Tile Inc.

Photo courtesy of Trade Commission of Spain

(far left) **White on white** *makes a dramatic visual statement. The crisp white countertop tiles are defined and made more visually dramatic by the wide, white grout lines.*

(left) **Decorative trim tiles** *give this countertop tile installation an attractive edge. Lighter-colored tiles are used to define the work area on the top of the counter. Matching wall tiles are installed on an adjacent wall, at an angle, to distinguish between the two separate surfaces.*

Photo courtesy of LATCO Products

(left) **A sea of small blue ceramic tiles** *inspires an aquatic theme in this spacious bathroom and spa. The water-resistant qualities of the tiles make them ideal for every application in the room.*

Counter Tiles

Hand-painted trim tiles *border this countertop and reflect the painted design in the porcelain sink. The decorative design is also used on the walls and as a border around the mirror.*

Stylishly shaped trim tiles *and accent tiles with a delicate decorative design add a light, fresh look to this pastel powder room.*

Contrasting colored grout *defines the grid and makes it a decorative element in this countertop. The braided trim tile along the backsplash adds a distinctive design element to the water-resistant surface of the countertop.*

Coordinated tile sets *offer matching tiles for flat surfaces, edges and accents. This beautiful bathroom reflects the elegance ceramic tile is capable of bringing to a bathroom or any other setting.*

Beige and black with accents of brass are the colors that comprise this sophisticated ceramic tile countertop. The metallic gold accent tile picks up the brass in the fixtures and frame of the mirror on the wall behind. Besides the wonderfully rich aesthetic quality, ceramic tile has the advantage of being water-resistant as well.

Designing With Tile

The ideal ceramic or natural tile design delivers the perfect balance between functional needs and aesthetic pleasure. This is not difficult to achieve if you research the characteristics of the various types of tile and follow the basic rules of shape, size, color, texture, scale, pattern and rhythm. The vast selection of ceramic and natural tiles available offers a range of composition possibilities that is almost endless. By rearranging the basic building blocks of design you can compose a well-planned ceramic tile configuration that organizes the different parts of a space into one harmonious whole.

Begin planning your tile design by compiling examples of ceramic tile design schemes from books and magazines. Also collect paint, wallpaper and fabric samples that will need to coordinate with your ceramic tile design. Visit a tile showroom to see examples of tile types you are considering. Ask for samples to take home

with you so you can view the tile in the proposed setting. Because of the durability and longevity of ceramic tile, you will probably be living with your selection for a long time, so choose colors and designs that will allow you to replace the furnishings or change the motif of the room.

Although grout is not considered as part of the design of the tile, it plays an important part in the overall look of a ceramic tile application. There are two design factors that you need to think about when selecting grout—the color and the width of the joint, or the space between tiles. Using a grout color that contrasts with the tiles will emphasize the grid pattern that forms as a result of the spacing between the tiles and the geometry of the design. This can create a stunning look, if done correctly. However, it will also make any flaws or irregularities in width or placement more prominent. To decrease the emphasis on the grid, choose a grout that matches the tile colors or one that will be almost neutral when compared to the tile. If you are installing decorative tiles, match the grout color to the background color, otherwise the grout will compete with the design for attention.

(opposite page) **Clever ceramic tile patterns** *allow you to create a tiled wall that looks like wallpaper. But the ceramic tile is water-resistant, washable and will last much longer.*

(left) **This all-white ensemble of ceramic floor** *tiles uses texture and patterns, as well as the contrast between glossy and matte tiles, to create the subtle visual styling of this tile application.*

Photo courtesy of Crossville Ceramics. Photo above courtesy of Ann Sacks Tile & Stone

Shape & Size

One of the primary principals of design is the way the shape and size of various elements in a design scheme relate to one another within the space. These elements should balance and complement each other. The size and shape of tiles used in various applications can also affect the feel, or ambience, of a room. For example, circular elements give a room a feeling of closure that can be comforting. Curved shapes help emphasize areas that you want to define, such as a shower area within a large bathroom. The most common tile shape available is square. Square tiles are the most versatile and the easiest to install. Other common shapes include rectangles, hexagons and octagons. Shape can also be accentuated with color. By using borders, stripes and contrasting colors, you can create dramatic shapes using square tiles.

The basic rule to follow when dealing with size in relation to ceramic tile application is—small tiles look good in small rooms and large tiles look better in large rooms. Large tiles tend to expand the size of the surface; small tiles tend to decrease it. If you are using more than one size tile in the same room, use large tiles on lower surfaces rather than on higher ones. Avoid tiling a countertop with tiles that are larger than the ones on the floor; this will make the room look awkward and top-heavy.

Photo courtesy of Monarch Tile Inc.

Decorative wall and trim tiles *add a colorful border around this inset alcove. The contrasting-colored tiles have a distinctive narrow rectangular shape that helps create a contrasting border that defines the shelf area.*

Photo courtesy of Marcia Corona, Italian Trade Commission - Tile Center in New York

Large ceramic floor tiles *expand the sense of space and add a water-resistant surface to this work area. The diagonal application enhances this sense of roominess. Smaller-sized tiles, on the walls and counter areas, contrast nicely with the larger floor tiles. Because there is more tiled area on the walls and counters, the smaller tiles are used here. Larger tiles, such as those used on the floor, would overwhelm the entire room.*

Custom tile designers use a multitude of shapes, colors and sizes when creating an original tile design. This one-of-a-kind design will add originality and a handcrafted appeal to any setting.

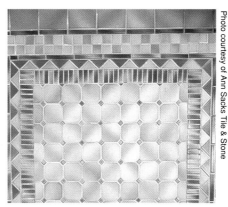

Color, size and shape all play an intricate part in this ceramic tile pattern.

A delicate floral design made from relief tile creates this ceramic tile border. The pattern is accentuated by the colorful glaze that has been applied.

Colors have a dramatic effect in this luxurious lavatory. The matching grout used on the marbled white tiles gives the tiled areas a larger unified look. When used with darker tiles, the light-colored grout lines define the tiles and make them look smaller.

An original floor tile design turns this marble floor into a modern-day masterpiece. The centerpiece of the design is a configuration that creates the illusion of an area rug in the center of the room. Pieces of tile resembling mosaic tiles are inset randomly throughout the floor pattern.

Color

Color is the most influential element of basic design. The vast selection and intensity of colors available is one of the strongest advantages of ceramic tile. Color sets the mood in a setting—you feel color as well as see it. Color selection is very important to establishing the ambience of a room. Ceramic tiles are available in almost any color imaginable, and tile manufacturers regularly adjust their color selections to match current fashion trends. If you can't find the color you're looking for in a manufactured tile, custom colors can be created; ask your local tile distributor for details.

You can install colored tiles in a defined pattern, or place them randomly. The number of colors you put together in one design depends on the other elements in a room, such as the furniture, wallpaper and window treatments. The colors in your tile design must work with all of the design components in a setting. A monochromatic, or one-color, design scheme can have a soothing effect, but may become too monotonous. Analogous, or closely related, colors are always a safe combination. Complementary or contrasting colors intensify

one another. A multicolored design adds excitement, but can be too busy if overdone.

The placement of colors in relation to one another, and to the other elements in a room, affects the way they are perceived. Warm colors are comfortable and cozy, and make objects seem closer. Cool colors are refreshing and clean; they give the illusion of receding. The best interior design schemes combine both warm and cool colors and allow one color temperature to dominate. Light colors make a space seem larger, while darker colors minimize space. Dark floors can make a large room seem smaller and more intimate. A dark floor will help light furnishings stand out more, while a light floor will make the room seem larger and will help light furnishings blend into the overall design scheme.

Bold colors work best in small doses in smaller areas, such as entries or hallways. If an area has an alcove or niche that is an interesting focal point, it can be highlighted with a dramatic tile design.

Photo above courtesy of Selene Seltzer/Designs in Tile, Mt. Shasta, CA
This photo courtesy of Sicis, Italian Trade Commission - Tile Center in New York

A sense of motion and excitement is created when complementary colors are used in conjunction with the right shapes. This tile application, featuring a beautiful six-pointed ceramic tile star, seems to radiate rings of blue hues from aqua to cobalt.

(above) **The natural tone** of the wood cabinetry is complemented by the natural muted colors used in the ceramic tile accents on the wall behind the counter and across the front of the hood above the stove.

(left) **The soft colors** and rounded shape of the small ceramic tiles create the ambience of a textured area rug. Distinctive borders, made with narrow green tiles, help define the areas of the floor and reinforce the area rug illusion.

31

The hint of a checkerboard pattern *adds an interesting accent to this lavish bathroom. The diagonal diamond pattern is repeated in the floor pattern of contrasting white grout and large rust and teal tiles.*

Designing with tile

Pattern & Texture

Pattern and texture also contribute to the development of a decorating theme. Ceramic and natural tile adds a great deal of interest and character to any room; it can be matte, textured, patterned or sculptured, depending on the mood you're trying to create. Smooth textures and precise patterns create a more formal setting, while rough and random patterns are more suited to casual settings. Texture also affects the look of any color. Smooth surfaces will appear lighter and rough ones darker.

Ceramic tile can help reconfigure spaces. Tiles set in a diagonal pattern can change the perceived dimensions of a room, while curved or circular patterns add a feeling of openness and flow to a space. Repeating colors in a pattern and using the same colors in more than one area of a setting is another way to unify a look. You can create optical illusions by laying tile in different patterns or contrasting colors. Tile can be used to define individual areas in a room by using borders or changing colors.

Small, triangular-shaped tiles *create a lively diamondlike pattern of turquoise and black that pops against the sparkling white ceramic. Combining the small tiles with the contrasting white grout creates a textured, almost quilted effect.*

Blue and white Italian ceramic tiles *bring a taste of the old country to this kitchen. On the floor, small tiles create patterns that resemble one large floor tile. Each design is framed by solid white tiles, which reinforce the illusion of larger floor tiles and keep the space from feeling too crowded.*

The dominant white *of this bathroom is set off by the bold red checkerboard pattern and the thin green trim tiles. The vivid colors accentuate the ledge and make it seem larger than it really is.*

Planning this unusual pattern *took thought and imagination. The soothing shades of green and unusual tile shapes create an example of the unique pattern possibilities you can achieve working with ceramic tile.*

Artistic Expressions

Ceramic tile adds a unique personality to a space, and is one of the best ways to customize a home with a design element. Art tiles function to provide specialized graphic elements and options. Different types of art tiles include: decorated tiles, such as hand-painted and tiles with decals applied; mosaic tiles; relief tiles and tiles cut from natural stone. Art tiles are ideal for aesthetic applications, but are not as strong and durable as ceramic tiles made for walls and floors.

Hand-painted tiles are often created for tile shops by artists. Although most hand-painted tiles are made by professionals, you can paint your own and have them fired and glazed. They come in an array of decorative designs and can be used as individual accents in a variety of places, such as the backsplash behind a kitchen sink or interspersed within a solid color border that runs along a wall. Entire scenes can be painted on a group of tiles.

Mosaic tiles are some of the most colorful and versatile types of tile. These smaller, decoratively shaped tiles look striking in any setting. Mosaic tiles can be made of natural clay tile or hard porcelain tile, in either glazed or unglazed versions.

Tiles are not only made from fired clay, they are also made from other natural materials, like stone, slate and marble. Natural tiles create a comfortable, unique ambience in any setting.

Trend-setting ceramic tiles can help you achieve affordable elegance in any area. In this beautiful bathroom, dark green wall tiles with a marbleized high-gloss finish create a soothing ambience. Metallic gold decals were applied to matching green tiles, which were used to add attractive accents, as well as a border that is stylish and sophisticated.

(top) **Clever use of texture and pattern** create a crisp, clean-looking kitchen. White ceramic counter tiles are combined with rope accent tiles and thick tile grout lines to create a flurry of visual activity in a seemingly calm setting.

(inset) **The arched alcove** above the stove and the rounded corners are accentuated by rope-style trim tiles in a complementary dark green color.

(left) **A decal of a soft pastel pattern** was applied to narrow border tiles, to help create a soothing setting for a relaxing soak in the tub. The rope styling of the ceramic trim tiles adds an element of texture, as well as a subtle visual accent.

35

Decorated Tiles

In addition to being glazed, tiles can also be decorated. Some decorated tiles are hand-painted, others have decals applied to them. Common themes for decorated tiles are animals and plants. Many times local artists can be hired to paint tiles to match wallpaper, fabric or an original design or pattern.

Decorated tiles can also be used in many outdoor areas. They are ideal for spa and pool applications—a mural of a scenic landscape or a delightful abstract design of shapes and colors can have a dynamic impact on a poolside setting.

Photo courtesy of Florida Tile Industries, Inc.

High-gloss, hand-painted color *reinforces the relief image cast in the design of the tile. Decorative border tiles pick up the same colors used in the relief tile and carry them throughout the setting.*

The artistic value *of tiles is celebrated in this display of age-worn, hand-painted ceramic tiles.*

Photo courtesy of Vietri

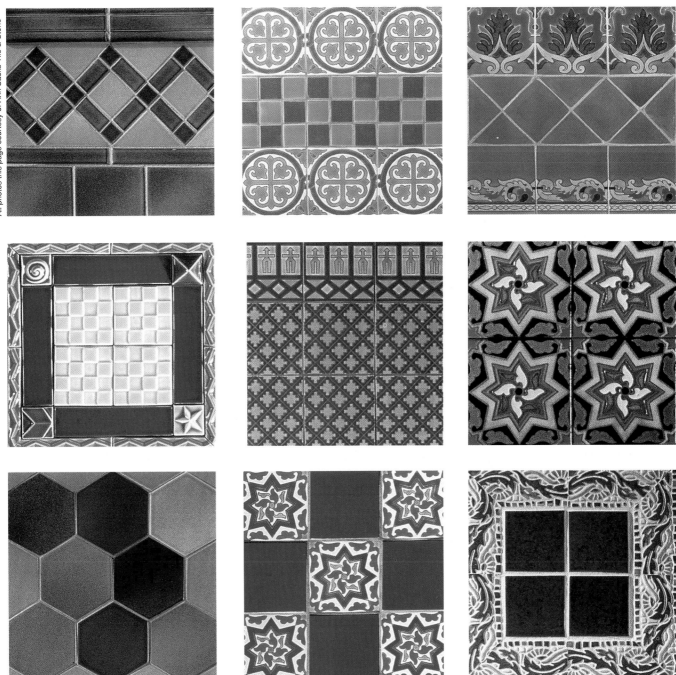

This amazing assortment of ceramic art tiles illustrates just a few of the many innovative options available today. A considerable impact can be achieved with a few decorated tiles. You can also combine large groups of matching, patterned tiles to create a wallpapered effect, which can also have a dramatic and stunning impact. Decorative tiles are appropriate in any entrance area, at the front or back of a house. They are also used to define the top or bottom edge of a dado. Decorative tiles also are an interesting backdrop for a display of china or glass.

Decorated Tiles

Hand-painted tiles are usually created for tile shops by local artists. You can also find hand-painted tiles at craft fairs and art shows. These one-of-a-kind creations are a great way to customize and add charm and personality to a kitchen or bar.

Hand-painted tiles can be set as individual accents in a backsplash wall or counter, or entire scenes can be painted on a group of tiles. Painted tiles are usually too fragile to be used in a floor installation but they are ideal as accents or installed in groups to form a pattern or scenic illustration.

Decal tiles are a less expensive alternative to hand-painted tile, yet they still have that special hand-finished quality and are just as attractive. Decals can be applied to almost any tiles; colored, patterned or plain. Hand-painting achieves the best results when used on plain tiles.

Common themes for decal tiles are flowers, animals, vegetables and graphic symbols. These images are permanently applied to the tiles through a firing process done at the tile store. Decal tiles are fragile, like painted tile, and should be used on wall applications and lightly used areas of countertops.

These hand-colored, multitile panels *create a scenic mural on this kitchen wall that resembles the painted tiles that adorned the walls of late 19th-century Europe. From this kitchen alcove, the realistic impact of this mural creates the illusion of looking out an actual window.*

Decorated tiles *can be used to great practical and decorative effect in many areas around the house. Kitchen and bathroom sinks need a backsplash to protect the wall behind them. A small panel of decorative tiles is one way to add interest to a backsplash. More delicate, decorated tiles can sometimes be used on the floor in small quantities, in areas that don't get heavy use. For example, on the floor in front of the sink, several decorated tiles are grouped together to create a mat effect. The patterned area should be wider and deeper than the actual sink.*

39

Natural Tiles

One type of tile that has gained recent popularity in interior design is natural tile. This type of tile is cut from natural stone, such as slate, marble and limestone. Modern sawing techniques have made natural stone widely available for domestic use. The thinner sliced stone is cheaper and lighter to transport and install.

Terra-cotta tiles are also called earthenware tiles. These handmade tiles have a more rustic look than quarry tiles, which are flatter and more regular in shape. The most significant difference between terra-cotta and quarry tile is the temperature they are fired at; quarry tiles are fired at a much higher temperature, so they are less porous than terra-cotta.

Natural tiles also add a textural contrast that increases their dramatic effect. Large natural tiles can add a sense of permanence and stability to a room. For example, large marble tiles used on both the entryway floor and the floors of the adjacent rooms can visually expand the space. Slate is another natural stone that can be used to create a hard-wearing and dramatic floor. It has a soft, rippling texture that adds an attractive touch and also helps prevent slipping.

Photo courtesy of Trade Commission of Spain

Massive buff and blue marble floor tiles *are laid on the diagonal. Wall tiles of the same marble extend the grace and grandeur of this Euro-style bathroom up the walls and into the hall.*

A terra-cotta tile floor is enlivened by small, patterned inset tiles. Terra-cotta is available in many color variations and shapes. The area the terra-cotta tiles originate from will determine the coloring of the tiles. Some shades are richer and darker, while others are softer and browner.

(inset) Terra-cotta tiles create a rustic, natural-looking floor. In this application, smaller terra-cotta tiles were given a decorative decal and used as a design accent.

Both bottom photos courtesy of Florida Tile Industries, Inc.

The rose-colored and buff-colored marble tiles *impart a formal ambience in this sitting area. Inlaid pieces of the buff-colored marble are used to create an intricate border.*

Natural Tiles

Many types of natural stone are suitable for both indoor and outdoor use. Natural stone makes a good surface for outdoor terraces and patios, as well as porches, conservatories, kitchens and hallways. When used in both interior and exterior settings, natural stone tiles can help make the transition between the interior space and the outdoors smooth and graceful.

When installing natural tile outdoors, take into account the climactic conditions of the setting, especially if the climate includes days with freezing temperatures. You can seal natural stone and slate tiles to help preserve their original appearance.

Add textural interest *to a monochromatic natural tile application with sculpted tile borders of natural-looking ceramic. The natural stone, as well as the ceramic tiles, impart water-resistant protection to the wall and exude a warm ambience.*

A sunny, poolside patio *is surfaced with water-resistant terra-cotta tiles. The rough surface of the natural tiles creates a safer, slip-resistant surface for this outdoor wet area.*

The provincial look *of this terra-cotta floor is embellished with a decorative accent tile in every corner.*

All photos this page courtesy of Ann Sacks Tile & Stone

The uneven textures and muted, earthy colors *of natural stone are captured in the rustic look of these tiles. Natural-finish tiles can be used for various purposes and effects. Marble tiles appear luxurious, and they're also very hard-wearing. Unglazed terra-cotta imparts interesting tones and textures to a surface. Natural tiles are individually shaped and look as though they were cut by hand. Their subtle color variations add to the authenticity of the look and charm.*

Mosaic Tiles

A mosaic design is the combination of small pieces of multicolored materials such as clay, marble, ceramic or glass, which are fired for a long time at a high temperature. Mosaic tiles are very dense and hard, and can withstand freezing. The small pieces are known as tesserae and the labor of assembling them into a pattern or picture is the difficult and costly aspect of mosaic work. The most common shapes of mosaic tiles are squares, octagons and hexagons—special original designs are also available. Generally, mosaic tiles are sold back-mounted on mesh sheets.

The number of mosaic floors that have survived intact, in entryways, halls, porches and pathways, is a testimony to the toughness and longevity of the material. Mosaic tiles are used to create intricate and elaborate designs. At its most detailed, a mosaic can be almost like a painting. The well-defined, sophisticated look of a mosaic design can often stand by itself as a unique work of art.

Mosaics are good for walls, floors, countertops and many other tile applications. They can be used both indoors and out, and in wet and dry locations. Mosaic tiles are especially effective in entryways, alcoves and other small areas where the brilliant colors and the intricacy

of a mosaic design become a visual focal point. Around fireplaces, they can add a striking design to a fireplace setting. Mosaic tile applied around a fireplace will also protect the tiled areas from stray sparks.

Mosaic tiles can be arranged in swirling and circular lines, presenting endless design and color possibilities. You can achieve dramatic results when mosaic tile is applied as a border design, in long, unbroken stretches, where the motion and rhythm of the design can gain momentum.

(right) **This intricately laid** *mosaic tile floor has the appearance of a rich Persian floor rug. The design uses small tiles to create a delicate floral design over this entire floor area.*

This photo courtesy of WALKER-ZANGER. Photo above courtesy of Selene Seltzer/Designs in Tile, Mt. Shasta, CA

(above) **These exuberant patterns** are modern examples of mosaic tile designs. Each tile contains several pieces of colored stone, and the process of making mosaic tiles is as labor-intensive today as it was centuries ago.

(left) **Very small ceramic tiles** have a visual impact similar to true mosaic tiles, when applied as a surface to the floor and sides of the tub in this small bathroom setting.

Remove old wall surfaces in small sections, using a reciprocating saw. Cutting ceramic tile walls into sections is easier than chipping away individual tiles. For general safety, shut off electrical power and water supply lines, and check for pipes and wires before cutting into any wall.

Damaged framing members may be concealed by water-damaged wall or floor surfaces. If any portion of wall surface shows peeling, discoloration, or bowing, remove the entire surface to examine the framing members. Repair or reinforce damaged framing members before installing new wall surfaces.

Removing Wall & Floor Surfaces

Removing and replacing wall and floor surfaces has two main benefits. First, the access to wall cavities makes it much easier to update or expand bathroom plumbing and electrical systems. Second, removing surfaces lets you check the framing members behind walls and under floors for water damage and warping.

Do not try to install a new wall surface, such as ceramic tile, over old plaster or wallboard. This practice may seem to save time, but by concealing possible structural problems inside the walls, it actually may create more work in the long run.

Everything You Need:

Tools: reciprocating saw, long-handled floor scraper, pry bar, masonry chisel, masonry hammer, heat gun, putty knives, utility knife.

Materials: trisodium phosphate (TSP).

Tips for Removing Wall & Floor Surfaces

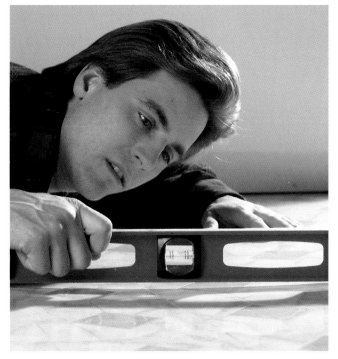

Inspect walls and floors for signs of warping or water damage before you remove the surfaces. Drag a long straightedge across the floor or wall to help detect valleys and bulges in the surface, which indicate that your wall or floor may have structural problems (see pages 52 and 53 for repair tips).

Pry off trim and molding. Loosen long pieces of trim a little at a time to prevent splintering. Use blocking between the pry bar and the wall to increase leverage. Label trim pieces as they are removed so you can reattach them properly.

Wear protective equipment when removing old wall and floor surfaces. Protective equipment should include a particle mask, eye protection, hearing protection, long-sleeved shirt, gloves, and sturdy shoes.

Use a masonry chisel and masonry hammer to chip away ceramic floor tile. Chipping away tiles makes it easier to cut the mortar bed and any underlayment into small sections for removal (page 48).

How to Remove Ceramic Wall Tile

1 Knock a small starter hole in the bottom of the wall, using a masonry hammer and masonry chisel. Be sure the floor is covered with a heavy tarp, and electricity and water are shut off.

2 Begin cutting out small sections of wall by inserting a reciprocating saw with a bimetal blade into the hole, and cutting along grout lines. Be careful when sawing near pipes and wiring.

3 Cut the entire wall surface into small sections, removing each section as it is cut.

How to Remove Ceramic Floor Tile

Ceramic tile set in adhesive: Chip away tile, using a masonry hammer and masonry chisel, then use a long-handled floor scraper to scrape away tile fragments and old adhesive residue. A floor sander may be used to create a smooth finish on the subfloor.

Ceramic tile set in mortar: Chip away tile, using a masonry hammer and chisel. Cut the old subfloor into small sections, using a circular saw with an old carbide blade. Pry up individual sections of floor with a wrecking bar. NOTE: If the old tile was laid on underlayment, raise the blade of the saw so it cuts through underlayment and mortar, but not subfloor.

How to Remove Vinyl Floor Tiles

1 Soften flooring adhesive by warming tiles with a heat gun. Wear eye protection and gloves.

2 Pry up tiles with a putty knife or a wallboard knife, then use the knife to scrape old adhesive residue off the underlayment or the subfloor.

3 Remove stubborn tile adhesive with a long-handled floor scraper.

How to Remove Sheet-vinyl Flooring

1 Remove baseboards, then cut the old flooring into 10"-wide strips, using a utility knife or a flooring knife. Cut through both the flooring and backing.

2 Remove the flooring strip by strip. Wrap one end around a rolling pin or piece of tubing, then roll up the strip of flooring material.

3 Scrape away any remaining backing or adhesive, using a long-handled floor scraper. When needed, use a trisodium phosphate (TSP) solution to loosen residue. Wear rubber gloves.

49

Remove underlayment and floor covering as if they were a single layer. This is an effective removal strategy with any floor covering that is bonded to the underlayment.

Removing Underlayment

Flooring contractors routinely remove the under-layment along with the floor covering before installing new flooring. This saves time and makes it possible to install new underlayment ideally suited to the new flooring. Do-it-yourselfers using this technique should make sure they cut flooring into manageable pieces that can be easily handled.

Warning: This floor removal method releases flooring particles into the air. Be sure the vinyl you are removing does not contain asbestos.

Everything You Need:

Tools: eye protection, circular saw, reciprocating saw, wood chisel, hand maul, masonry chisel, pry bar.

Removal Tip

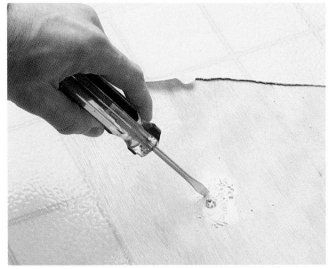

Examine fasteners to see how the underlayment is attached. Use a screwdriver to expose the heads of the fasteners. If the underlayment has been screwed down, you will need to remove the floor covering before you can unscrew the underlayment.

How to Remove Underlayment

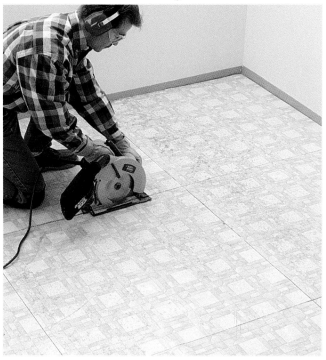

1 Adjust the cutting depth of a circular saw to equal the combined thickness of your floor covering and underlayment. Using a carbide-tipped blade, cut the floor covering and underlayment into squares measuring about 3 ft. square. Be sure to wear safety goggles and gloves.

VARIATION: If your existing floor is ceramic tile over plywood underlayment, use a hand maul and masonry chisel to chip away tile along cutting lines before making cuts.

2 Use a reciprocating saw to extend cuts close to the edges of walls. Hold the blade at a slight angle to the floor, and try not to damage walls or cabinets. Use a wood chisel to complete cuts near cabinets.

3 Separate underlayment from subfloor, using a flat pry bar and hammer. Remove and discard the sections of underlayment and floor covering immediately, watching for exposed nails.

Refasten loose subfloor material. Before installing new underlayment and floor covering, refasten any sections of loose subfloor to floor joists using deck screws.

Repairing Subfloors

A solid, securely fastened subfloor minimizes floor movement and ensures that your new floor will last a long time. After removing old underlayment, inspect the subfloor for loose seams, moisture damage, cracks, and other flaws. If your subfloor is made of dimensional lumber rather than plywood, you can use plywood to patch damaged sections; if the plywood patch does not quite match the height of the subfloor, use floor leveler to raise its surface to the correct height.

Everything You Need:

Tools: basic hand tools, flat trowel, drill with phillips head, circular saw, cat's paw.

Materials: floor leveler, 2" deck screws, plywood, 2 x 4 lumber.

Repair Tip

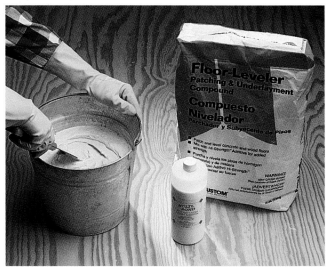

Floor leveler is used to fill in dips and low spots in plywood subfloors. Using a latex or acrylic additive, mix the leveler according to the manufacturer's directions.

How to Apply Floor Leveler

1 Fill dips, chips, or cracks in the subfloor with floor leveler. Mix leveler according to manufacturer's directions, then spread it on the subfloor with a trowel.

2 Check with a straightedge to make sure the filled area is even with the surrounding area; if not, apply more leveler. Allow leveler to dry, then shave off any ridges with the edge of a trowel, or sand smooth, if necessary.

How to Replace a Section of Subfloor

1 Mark, cut, and remove damaged areas. Mark a rectangle around the damage, with two sides centered over floor joists. Cut, using a circular saw with the blade adjusted to cut only through the subfloor. Use a chisel to complete cuts near walls.

2 Remove damaged section, then nail two 2 × 4 blocks between joists, centered under the cut edges for added support. If possible, end-nail blocks from below; otherwise toe-nail them from above.

3 Measure the cut-out section, then cut to fit, using material the same thickness as the original subfloor. Fasten to joists and blocks, using 2" deck screws spaced about 5" apart.

Install new plywood underlayment to provide the best possible base for gluing down resilient flooring or ceramic tile. Cut the plywood to fit around moldings and other room contours.

Installing Underlayment

When installing underlayment, make sure it is securely attached to the subfloor in all areas, including below all movable appliances. Notching the underlayment to properly fit room contours is often to most challenging step. Take time to measure carefully and transfer the correct measurements onto your underlayment. Rather than notching around door casings, you can undercut the casings and insert the underlayment beneath them.

Everything You Need:

Tools: basic hand tools; drill with phillips bit, circular saw, wallboard knife, power sander (for plywood); countersink drill bit (for high-density fiberboard); jig saw with carbide blade (for cementboard); ¼" notched trowel (for cementboard); ⅛" notched trowel, linoleum roller (for isolation membrane).

Materials: underlayment; 1" deck screws, latex patching compound (for plywood and high-density); dry-set mortar (for cementboard and isolation membrane).

How to Install Plywood Underlayment

1 Begin installing full sheets of plywood along the longest wall, making sure underlayment seams are not aligned with subfloor seams. Fasten plywood to the subfloor, using 1" screws driven every 6" along the edges and at 8" intervals throughout the rest of the sheet.

2 Continue fastening plywood to the subfloor, driving screw heads slightly below the underlayment surface. Leave ¼" expansion gaps at the walls and between sheets. Offset seams in subsequent rows.

3 Using a circular saw or jig saw, notch underlayment sheets to meet existing flooring in doorways, then fasten notched sheets to the subfloor.

4 Mix floor patching compound and latex or acrylic additive, according to manufacturer's directions. Then, spread it over seams and screw heads with a wallboard knife.

5 Let patching compound dry, then sand patched areas smooth, using a power sander.

1 Mix thin-set mortar according to manufacturer's recommendations. Starting at the longest wall, spread mortar on subfloor in a figure-eight pattern with a ¼" notched trowel. Spread only enough mortar for one sheet at a time. Set the cementboard sheet on the mortar, smooth-face up, making sure the edges are offset from subfloor seams.

2 Fasten cementboard to subfloor, using 1½" deck screws driven every 6" along edges and 8" throughout sheet; drive screw heads flush with surface. Continue spreading mortar and installing sheets along the wall. OPTION: If installing fiber/cement underlayment, use a ³⁄₁₆" notched trowel to spread mortar, and drill pilot holes for all screws.

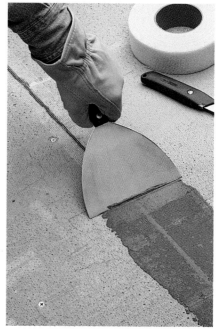

3 Cut cementboard pieces to fit, leaving a slight gap at the joints. For straight cuts, score a line with a utility knife, then snap the board along the score.

4 To cut holes, notches, or irregular shapes, use a jig saw with a carbide blade. Continue installing cementboard sheets to cover the entire floor.

5 Place fiberglass mesh tape over seams, and spread a thin layer of thin-set mortar over the tape with a wallboard knife, feathering the edges. Allow mortar to cure for two days before proceeding with tile installation.

How to Install Isolation Membrane

1 Thoroughly clean the subfloor, then apply thin-set mortar with a ⅛" notched trowel. Start spreading the mortar along a wall in a section as wide as the membrane, and 8 to 10 ft. long. NOTE: For some membranes, you must use a bonding material other than mortar. Read the directions on the label.

2 Roll out the membrane over the mortar. Cut the membrane to fit tightly against the walls, using a straightedge and utility knife.

3 Starting in the center of the membrane, use a linoleum roller to smooth out the surface toward the edges. This frees trapped air and presses out excess bonding material.

4 Repeat steps 1 through 3, cutting membrane as necessary at the walls, until the floor is completely covered with membrane. Do not overlap seams, but make sure they are tight. Allow mortar to cure for two days before installing tile.

Cut cementboard by scoring the fiberglass surface along cutting line, using a cementboard scoring tool or a utility knife. Snap the panel along the scored line, then cut the back surface (inset).

Installing Cementboard & Wallboard

Installing the appropriate wall surface helps ensure that your new walls last as long as possible. Install new wall surfaces only after you have checked the wall for any structural damage and made repairs, and an inspector has approved all new plumbing and wiring. If bathroom walls are not plumb and square, shim out the studs to ensure that the new wall surface will be flat and straight.

Cementboard and wallboard panels must be supported by studs along the edges. Cut the panels to fit available spaces, or install extra studs to provide surfaces for attaching panels.

Everything You Need:

Tools: utility knife, cementboard scoring tool, chalk, drill, jig saw, screwdriver, hammer, wallboard knife.

Materials: cardboard, fiberglass wallboard tape, wallboard screws and nails, wallboard corner bead, wallboard compound.

Wall Materials for Bathrooms

Choose wall materials appropriate for the moisture levels they must withstand. Standard wallboard (A) is made from a gypsum mineral layer covered with paper on both sides. It can be used in all areas that are not directly exposed to moisture. Water-resistant wallboard (B) is also made from gypsum, but has a water-resistant facing. Use it in wet areas, like behind sinks, and as a backer for tub surrounds or shower panels. Cementboard (C) is a rigid material with a cement core that is faced on both sides with fiberglass. Water does not damage cementboard, making it the best backing material for ceramic tile.

How to Install Wallboard or Cementboard Panels

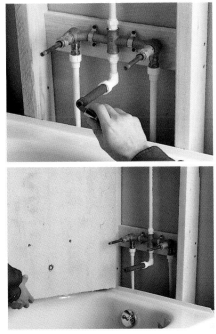
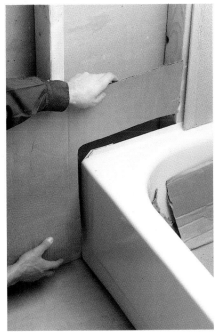

1 Mark panels for cutouts by coating ends of pipes and edges of electric boxes with chalk or lipstick (top). Position panel, then press it against the pipes to transfer marks (bottom). Make cutouts with a hole saw or jig saw.

2 Make a template from cardboard or heavy paper cut to fit irregular spaces. Use the template to mark cementboard or wallboard panels for cutting, then make cutouts with a jig saw.

3 Attach panels to wall studs with wallboard screws (drill pilot holes in cementboard). Screws should be driven along all panel edges and in the interior wall studs.

4 Cover all seams with fiberglass joint tape. NOTE: If the cementboard or water-resistant wallboard will be used as a backer for tub or shower surround panels, no taping is required.

Finishing wallboard surfaces: Attach metal corner bead to outside corners of wallboard walls, using wallboard nails driven at 8" intervals (left). Apply a thin layer of wallboard compound to all wallboard joints (right) and to nail and screw heads. Let compound dry, sand joints and patches smooth, then wipe clean. The finished wallboard surface may be painted or covered with water-resistant wallcovering.

Ceramic Floor Tile

Ceramic tile includes a wide variety of hard flooring products made from molded clay. Although there are significant differences among the various types, they are all installed using cement-based mortar as an adhesive and grout to fill the gaps between tiles. These same techniques can be used to install tiles cut from natural stone, like granite and marble.

Tile is the hardest of all flooring materials. With few exceptions, it is also the most expensive. But its durability makes it well worth the extra cost.

To ensure a long-lasting tile installation, the underlayment must be solid. Cementboard (or the thinner fiber/cementboard) is the best underlayment, since it has excellent stability and resists moisture. However, in rooms where moisture is not a factor, plywood is an adequate underlayment, and is considerably cheaper.

Many ceramic tiles have a glazed surface that protects the porous clay from staining. Unglazed ceramic tile should be protected with a sealer after it is installed. Grout sealers will prevent grout joints from trapping dirt and becoming discolored.

This section shows:
• Choosing Tile for Your Floor (pages 62 to 63)
• Tools & Materials (pages 64 to 65)
• Cutting Tile (pages 66 to 67)
• Installing Ceramic Tile (pages 68 to 75)

Ceramic tiles include several categories of products that are molded from clay, then baked in a kiln. *Glazed ceramic tile* is coated with a colored glaze after it is baked, then is fired again to produce a hard surface layer, which is clearly visible when the tile is viewed along the edges. *Quarry tile* is an unglazed, porous tile that is typically softer and thicker than glazed tiles. *Porcelain mosaic tile* is extremely dense and hard, and is naturally water-resistant. Like quarry tiles, porcelain tiles have the same color throughout their thickness when viewed along the edges. Porcelain tiles are often sold in mosaic sheets with a fiber or paper backing.

Natural-stone tiles are cut from stone extracted from quarries around the world. They are easily identified by visible saw marks at the edges and by their mineral veins or spots. Granite and marble tiles are generally sold with polished and sealed surfaces. Slate tiles are formed by cleaving the stone along natural faults, rather than by machine-cutting, giving the tiles an appealing, textured look. Stone tile can be prohibitively expensive for large installations, but can be used economically as an accent in highly visible areas.

Choosing Tile for Your Floor

A quality tile installation can last for decades, so make sure to choose colors and designs that will have long-lasting appeal. Be wary of trendy styles that may look dated in few years.

The time and labor required to install and maintain tile can also influence your decision. Square tiles have fewer grout lines and are therefore easier to maintain.

Square tiles come in many sizes. Commonly available sizes range from 6" to 12". Larger tiles can be installed relatively quickly and require less maintenance; they can also make a room look larger.

Irregular tile shapes include rectangles, hexagons, and octagons. Spaces between irregular tiles are often filled with smaller diamond or square-shaped tiles.

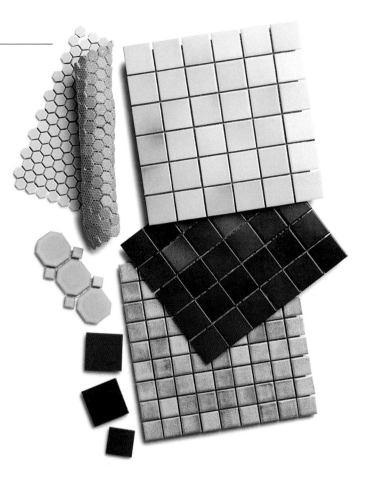

Mosaic tiles come in unglazed porcelain and glazed ceramic varieties. They are held together and installed in sheets with paper gauze backing or plastic webbing. Mosaic tiles come in a variety of sizes and shapes, though the most common forms are 1" and 2" squares.

Accent tiles, including mosaic borders and printed glazed tiles, can be used as continuous borders or placed individually among the other tiles.

Thin-set mortar is a fine-grained cement product used to bond floor tile to underlayment. It is prepared by adding liquid a little at a time to the dry materials and stirring the mixture to achieve a creamy consistency. Some mortars include a latex additive in the dry mix, but with others you will need to add liquid latex additive when you prepare the mortar.

Tools & Materials

The tools required to cut tiles and to apply mortar and grout are generally small and fairly inexpensive.

Materials needed for a tile installation include: adhesive thin-set mortar, used to fasten the tiles to the underlayment; grout, used to fill the joints between tiles; and sealers, used to protect the tile surface and grout lines. Make sure to use the materials recommended by the tile manufacturer.

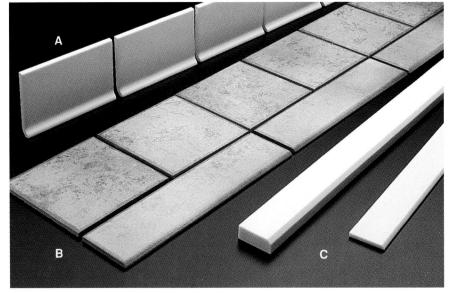

Trim and finishing materials for tile installations include base-trim tiles (A) which fit around the room perimeter, and bullnose tiles (B) used at doorways and other transition areas. Doorway thresholds (C) are made from synthetic materials as well as natural materials, such as marble, and come in thicknesses ranging from ¼" to ¾" to match different floor levels.

Tiling tools include adhesive-spreading tools, cutting tools, and grouting tools. Notched trowels (A) for spreading mortar come with notches of varying sizes and shapes; the size of the notch should be proportional to the size of the tile being installed. Cutting tools include a tile cutter (B), tile nippers (C), hand-held tile cutter (D), and jig saw with tungsten-carbide blade (E). Grouting tools include a grout float (F), grout sponge (G), buff rag (H), and foam brush (I). Other tiling tools include spacers (J), available in different sizes to create grout joints of varying widths; needle-nose pliers (K) for removing spacers; rubber mallet (L) for setting tiles into mortar; and caulk gun (M).

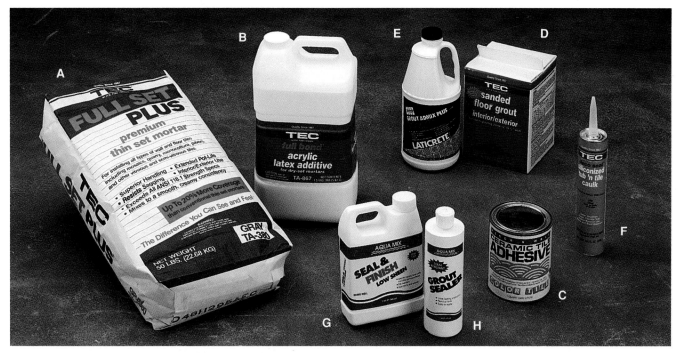

Tile materials include adhesives, grouts, and sealers. Thin-set mortar (A), the most common floor-tile adhesive, is often strengthened with latex mortar additive (B). Use wall-tile adhesive (C) for installing base-trim tile. Floor grout (D), is used to fill gaps between tiles; it is available in pretinted colors to match your tile. Grout can be made more resilient and durable with grout additive (E). Tile caulk (F) should be used in place of grout where tile meets another surface, like a bathtub. Porous tile sealer (G) and grout sealer (H) ward off stains and make maintenance easier.

Cutting Tile

Cutting tile accurately takes some practice and patience, but can be done effectively by do-it-yourselfers with the right tools.

Most cutting can be done with a basic tile cutter, such as the one shown on the opposite page. Tile cutters come in various configurations; each operates a little differently, though they all score and snap tile. Tile stores will often lend cutters to customers.

Other hand-held cutting tools are used to make small cuts or curved cuts.

Everything You Need:

Tools: wet saw, tile cutter, hand-held tile cutter, nippers, jig saw with tungsten-carbide blade.

Tile saws—also called wet saws because they use water to cool blades and tiles—are used primarily for cutting natural-stone tiles. They are also useful for quickly cutting notches in all kinds of hard tile. Wet saws are available for rent at tile dealers and rental shops.

Tips for Making Special Cuts

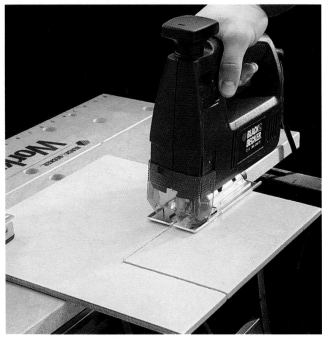

To make square notches, clamp the tile down on a worktable, then use a jig saw with a tungsten-carbide blade to make the cuts. If you need to cut many notches, a wet saw is more efficient.

To cut mosaic tiles, use a tile cutter to score tiles in the row where the cut will occur. Cut away excess strips of mosaics from the sheet, using a utility knife, then use a hand-held tile cutter to snap tiles one at a time. NOTE: Use tile nippers to cut narrow portions of tiles after scoring.

How to Make Straight Cuts in Ceramic Tile

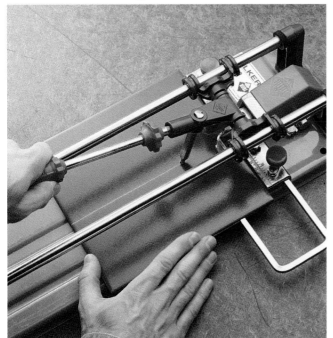

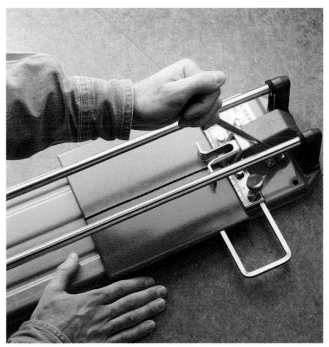

1 Mark a cutting line on the tile with a pencil, then place the tile in the cutter so the tile-cutting wheel is directly over the line. Pressing down firmly on the wheel handle, run the wheel across the tile to score the surface.

2 Snap the tile along the scored line, as directed by the tool manufacturer. Usually, snapping the tile is accomplished by depressing a lever on the tile cutter.

How to Make Curved Cuts with Tile Nippers

1 Mark a cutting line on the tile face, then use the scoring wheel of a hand-held tile cutter to score the cut line. Make several parallel scores, not more than ¼" apart, in the waste portion of the tile.

2 Use tile nippers to gradually remove the scored portion of the tile. TIP: To cut circular holes in the middle of a tile (step 9, pages 71), first score and cut the tile so it divides the hole in two, using the straight-cut method, then use the curved-cut method to remove waste material from each half of the hole.

Installing Ceramic Floor Tile

Ceramic tile installations start with the same steps as resilient tile projects: snapping perpendicular layout lines and dry-fitting tiles to ensure the best placement.

When you start setting tiles in thin-set mortar, work in small sections at a time so the mortar does not dry before the tiles are set. Also, plan your installation to avoid kneeling on set tiles.

Everything You Need:

Tools: basic hand tools, rubber mallet, tile cutter, tile nippers, hand-held tile cutter, needlenose pliers, grout float, grout sponge, soft cloth, small paint brush.

Materials: thin-set mortar, tile, tile spacers, grout, grout sealer, tile caulk.

How to Install Ceramic Floor Tile

1 Draw reference and layout lines, then mix a batch of thin-set mortar (page 64). Spread thin-set mortar evenly against both reference lines of one quadrant, using a ¼" square-notched trowel. Use the edge of the trowel to create furrows in the mortar bed.

Variation: For large tiles or uneven natural stone, use a larger trowel with notches that are at least ½" deep.

2 Set the first tile in the corner of the quadrant where the reference lines intersect. TIP: When setting tiles that are 8" square or larger, twist each tile slightly as you set it into position.

3 Using a soft rubber mallet, gently rap the central area of each tile a few times to set it evenly into the mortar.

VARIATION: For mosaic sheets, use a ³⁄₁₆" V-notched trowel to spread mortar, and use a grout float to press the sheets into the mortar.

4 To ensure consistent spacing between tiles, place plastic tile spacers at corners of the set tile. NOTE: With mosaic sheets, use spacers equal to the gaps between tiles.

(continued next page)

5 Position and set adjacent tiles into mortar along the reference lines. Make sure tiles fit neatly against the spacers. NOTE: Spacers are only temporary; be sure to remove them before the mortar hardens.

6 To make sure adjacent tiles are level with one another, lay a straight piece of 2 × 4 across several tiles at once, and rap the 2 × 4 with a mallet.

7 Lay tile in the remaining area covered with mortar. Repeat steps 1 to 6, continuing to work in small sections, until you reach walls or fixtures.

8 Measure and mark tiles for cutting to fit against walls and into corners. Cut tiles to fit (pages 66 to 67). Apply thin-set mortar directly to the back of the cut tiles instead of the floor, using the notched edge of the trowel to furrow the mortar.

9 Set cut pieces into position, and press down on them until they are level with adjacent tiles.

10 Measure, cut, and install tiles requiring notches or curves to fit around obstacles, such as exposed pipes or toilet drains.

11 Carefully remove spacers with needlenose pliers before the mortar hardens.

(continued next page)

12 Apply mortar and fill in tiles in remaining quadrants, completing one quadrant at a time before beginning the next. TIP: Before applying grout, inspect all of the tile joints and remove any high spots of mortar that could show through grout, using a utility knife or a grout knife.

13 Install threshold material in doorways. The most long-lasting thresholds are made from solid-surface mineral products. If the threshold is too long for the doorway, cut it to fit with a jig saw or circular saw and a tungsten-carbide blade. Set the threshold in thin-set mortar so the top is even with the tile. Keep the same space between the threshold as between tiles. Let the mortar cure for at least 24 hours.

14 Prepare a small batch of floor grout to fill tile joints. TIP: When mixing grout for porous tile, such as quarry or natural stone, use an additive with a release agent to prevent grout from bonding to the tile surfaces.

15 Starting in a corner, pour the grout over the tile. Use a rubber grout float to spread grout outward from the corner, pressing firmly on float to completely fill joints. For best results, tilt the float at a 60° angle to the floor and use a figure-eight motion.

16 Use the grout float to remove excess grout from the surface of the tile. Wipe diagonally across the joints, holding the float in a near-vertical position. Continue applying grout and wiping off excess until about 25 sq. ft. of the floor has been grouted.

17 Wipe a damp grout sponge diagonally over about 2 sq. ft. of the tile at a time to remove excess grout. Rinse the sponge in cool water between wipes. Wipe each area once only; repeated wiping can pull grout from the joints. Repeat steps 14 to 17 to apply grout to the rest of the floor.

18 Allow the grout to dry for about 4 hours, then use a soft cloth to buff the tile surface free of any remaining grout film.

(continued next page)

How to Install Ceramic Floor Tile (continued)

19 Apply grout sealer to the grout lines, using a small sponge brush or sash brush. Avoid brushing sealer on the tile surfaces. Wipe up any excess sealer immediately.

VARIATION: Use a tile sealer to seal porous tile, such as quarry tile or any unglazed tile. Roll a thin coat of sealer (refer to manufacturer's instructions) over the tile and grout joints with a paint roller and extension handle.

How to Install Base-trim Tile

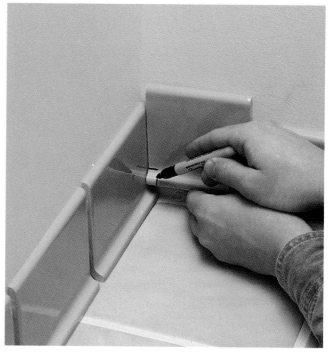

1 To give your new tiled floor a more professional look, install base-trim tiles at the bases of the walls. Start by dry-fitting the tiles to determine the best spacing (grout lines in base tile do not always align with grout lines in the floor tile). Use rounded "bullnose" tiles at outside corners, and mark tiles for cutting as needed.

2 Leaving a ⅛" expansion gap between tiles at corners, mark any contour cuts necessary to allow the coved edges to fit together. Use a jig saw with a tungsten-carbide blade to make curved cuts (see page 66).

3 Begin installing base-trim tiles at an inside corner. Use a notched trowel to apply wall adhesive to the back of the tile. Slip ⅛" spacers under each tile to create an expansion joint.

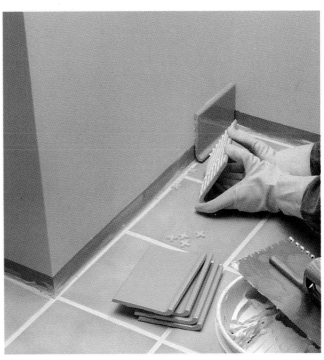

4 Press the tile into the adhesive. Continue setting tiles, using spacers to maintain ⅛" gaps between the tiles and an expansion joint between the tile and the floor.

5 At outside corners, use a double-bullnose tile on one side, to cover the edge of the adjoining tile.

6 After adhesive dries, grout the vertical joints between tiles, and apply grout along the tops of the tiles to make a continuous grout line. After grout cures, fill the expansion joint at the bottom of the tiles with caulk.

A diagonal floor pattern is easy to install once you establish reference lines at a 45° angle to the original layout lines. Installation is similar to that of ordinary square tile, except that trim cuts will be diagonal.

Advanced Floor Tile Techniques

Confident do-it-yourselfers familiar with basic tile techniques may be ready to undertake a project more challenging than a standard square tile floor installation. While the installations shown here usually require more time, the finished effect is well worth the extra effort.

For example, simply rotating the layout by 45° can yield striking results, as shown in the photo above. Offsetting the joints in adjacent tile rows to create a "running bond" pattern, a technique borrowed from masonry (opposite page), also adds visual

interest. A third technique features a unique geometrical look using hexagonal tile. The final project shown, installing a tile border, employs a combination of techniques to create the look of an elegant area rug, using tile.

The four advanced tile projects shown in this section assume a basic knowledge of tile installation techniques (pages 66 to 75). For this reason, this section focuses on layout issues specific to certain tile shapes or desired effects.

How to Lay a Running-bond Tile Pattern

1 Start a running-bond tile installation by dry-fitting tile in the standard manner to establish working reference lines. Dry-fit a few tiles side by side, using spacers to maintain proper joint spacing, and measure the total width of the dry-fitted section (A). Use this measurement to snap a series of equally spaced parallel lines to help keep your installation straight. Running-bond layouts are most effective with rectangular tiles.

2 Spread thin-set mortar and lay the first row of tiles starting at a point where the layout lines intersect. Offset the next row by a measurement equal to one-half the length of the tile.

3 Continue setting tiles, filling one quadrant at a time, using the parallel reference lines as guides to keep the rows straight. Immediately wipe off any mortar that falls on the tiles. When finished, allow the mortar to cure, then follow the steps for grouting and cleaning (page 73).

How to Lay Hexagonal Tile

1 Snap perpendicular reference lines on the underlayment, then lay out three or four tiles in each direction along the layout lines, using plastic spacers with one flange between the tiles to maintain even spacing. Measure the length of this layout in both directions (A, B). Use measurement A to snap a series of equally spaced parallel lines across the entire floor, then do the same for measurement B in the other direction.

2 Apply dry-set mortar and begin setting tile as with square tile (pages 68 to 74). Apply mortar directly to the undersides of any tiles that extend outside the mortar bed.

3 Continue setting tiles, using the grid layout and spacers to keep your work aligned. Wipe off any mortar that falls on the tile surfaces. When finished, allow the mortar to cure, then follow the steps for applying grout (pages 72 to 74).

How to Lay a Tile Border with a Diagonal Pattern

1 Snap perpendicular reference lines, then dry-fit border tiles in the planned area, using spacers. Make sure the border tiles are aligned with the reference lines. Next, dry-fit the tiles at the outside corners of the border arrangement. Adjust the tile positions to create a layout with minimal cutting (this will take some trial-and-error). When the layout of the tiles is set, snap chalk lines around the border tiles and trace the edges of the outside tiles. Install these tiles.

2 Install the field tiles inside the tile border. For an interesting visual effect, draw layout lines that are at a 45° angle from the perpendicular reference lines to create diagonal layout lines.

3 Use standard tile-setting techniques to fill in the field tiles in the inside border (pages 68 to 74, and 76). TIP: Kneel on a wide board to distribute your weight if you need to work in a tiled area that has not cured overnight.

Tiles at each end of the same wall should be cut to a similar size.

Layout adjusted so the row of accent tiles is unbroken by medicine cabinet.

Rows of trimmed tiles should be positioned near the top and bottom of tiled area to make them less obvious.

Tiles at each end of the same wall should be cut to a similar size.

Tiles above tub should be full-size or nearly full-size.

Good planning and careful work are the keys to achieving professional-looking results with ceramic wall tile. The tile project shown above was planned so the tiles directly above the most visible surface (in this bathroom, the bathtub) are nearly full height. To accomplish this, cut tiles were used in the second row up from the floor. The short second row also allows the row of accent tiles to run uninterrupted under the medicine cabinet. Cut tiles in both corners should be of similar width to preserve the symmetrical look of the room.

Installing Ceramic Wall Tile

Ceramic tile is a traditional, custom-installed material frequently used for bathroom walls, shower stalls, and floors. When properly installed, ceramic tile outlasts most other wall and floor coverings.

Tile is sold in a wide variety of colors, shapes, sizes, and finishes. For most projects, tiles that are at least 4 × 6 are easiest to install because they require less cutting and cover more surface area. Smaller tiles can form more intricate patterns and create safe, nonslip floor surfaces.

To ensure long-lasting results, remove the old wall surface down to the studs, and install a new base layer of cementboard (page 59).

Use a thin layer of dry-set mortar to create a bonding surface for ceramic wall tile. Avoid using the thick beds of standard mortar that were used to set wall tile for many years. Also avoid adhesives or mastics that have no mortar content, because these products do not work well on vertical surfaces.

Everything You Need:

Tools: marker, tape measure, carpenter's level, notched trowel, tile cutter, rod saw, drill with masonry bit, clamps, grout float, sponge, small paint brush, caulk gun.

Materials: straight 1 × 2, dry-set tile mortar with latex additive, ceramic wall tile, ceramic trim tile (as needed), tile grout with latex additive, tub & tile caulk, alkaline grout sealer.

Tips for Planning Tile Layouts

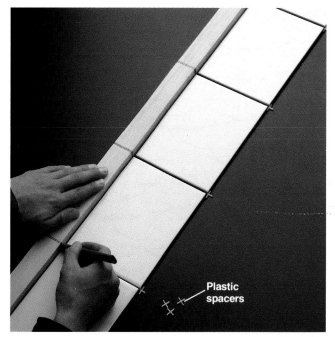

Use planning brochures and design catalogs to help you create decorative patterns and borders for your ceramic tile project. Brochures and catalogs are available free of charge from many tile manufacturers.

Make a tile stick to mark layout patterns on walls. To make a tile stick, set a row of tiles (and plastic spacers, if they will be used) in the selected pattern on a flat surface. Mark a straight 1 × 2 to match the tile spacing. Include any narrow trim tiles or accent tiles. If your tiles are square, you will need only one tile stick. For rectangular and odd-shaped tiles, make separate sticks for the horizontal and vertical layouts.

Materials for Tiling Projects

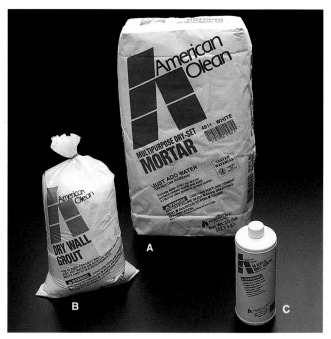

Ceramic tile types include: (A) mosaic tile sheets, (B) 4 × 4 glazed wall tiles with self-spacing edge lugs, (C) textured quarry tiles (natural stone) for floors, and (D) trim tiles for borders and accents.

Bonding materials for ceramic tile include: (A) dry-set mortar, (B) grout mix, and (C) latex grout additive. Latex additive makes grout lines stronger and more crack-resistant.

How to Mark a Layout for Wall Tile

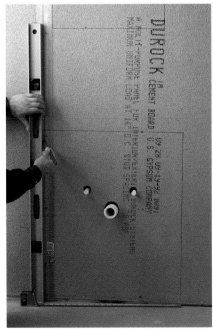

1 Mark the wall to show the planned location of all vanities, wall cabinets, recessed fixtures, and ceramic wall accessories, like soap and toothbrush holders or towel rods.

2 Locate the most visible horizontal line in the bathroom (usually the top edge of the bathtub). Measure up and mark a point at a distance equal to the height of one ceramic tile (if the tub edge is not level, measure up from the lowest spot). Draw a level line through this point, around the entire room. This line represents a tile grout line and is used as a reference line for making the entire tile layout.

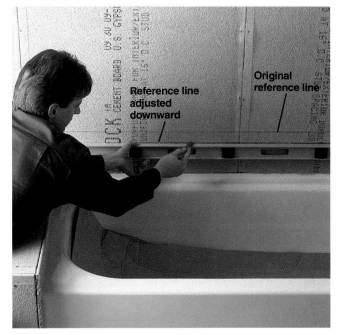

3 Use the tile stick to see how the tile pattern will run in relation to other features in the room, like countertops, window and door frames, and wall cabinets. Hold the tile stick so it is perpendicular to the horizontal reference line, with one joint mark touching the line, and note the location of tile joints.

4 Adjust the horizontal reference line if the tile stick shows that tile joints will fall in undesirable spots. In the bathroom shown above, adjusting the reference line downward allows an unbroken row of accent tiles to span the wall under the medicine cabinet (see photo, page 80).

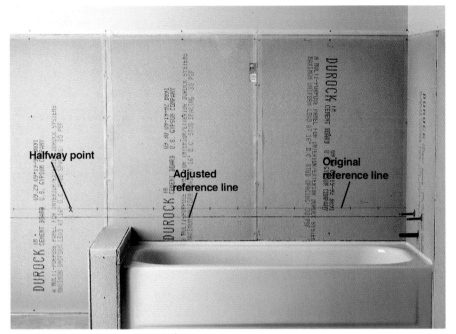

Labels on image: **Halfway point**, **Adjusted reference line**, **Original reference line**

5 On each wall, measure and mark the halfway point along the horizontal reference line (step 4). Using the tile stick as a guide, mark lines in each direction from the halfway point to show where the vertical grout joints will be located. If tile stick shows that corner tiles will be less than 1/2 of full tile width, adjust the layout as shown in next step.

6 Adjust the layout of vertical joints by moving the halfway point (step 5) 1/2 the width of a tile in either direction. Use a carpenter's level to draw a vertical reference line through this point, from the floor to the top tile row.

7 Use the tile stick to measure up from the floor along the vertical reference line, a distance equal to the height of one tile plus 1/8", and mark a point on the wall. Draw a level reference line through this point, across the wall.

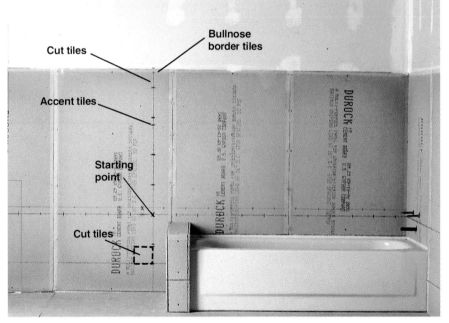

Labels on image: **Cut tiles**, **Bullnose border tiles**, **Accent tiles**, **Starting point**, **Cut tiles**

8 Mark reference lines to show where the remaining tile joints will be located, starting at the point where vertical and horizontal reference lines meet. Include any decorative border or accent tiles. If a row of cut tiles is unavoidable, position it near the floor, between the first and third rows, or at the top, near border tiles. Extend all horizontal reference lines onto adjoining walls that will be tiled, then repeat steps 5 to 8 for all other walls being tiled.

How to Install Ceramic Wall Tile

1 Mark layout pattern (pages 82 to 83), then begin installation with the second row of tiles from the floor. If layout requires cut tiles for this row, mark and cut tiles for the entire row at one time.

2 Make straight cuts with a tile cutter. Place the tile face up on the tile cutter, with one side flush against the cutting guide. Adjust the cutting tool to desired width, then score a groove by pulling the cutting wheel firmly across the tile. Snap the tile along the scored line, as directed by the tool manufacturer.

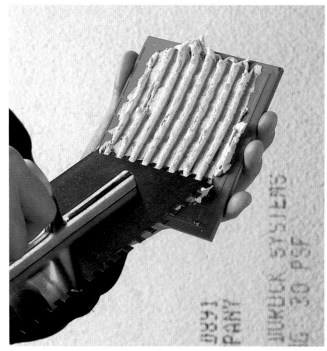

3 Mix a small batch of dry-set mortar containing a latex additive. (Some mortar has additive mixed in by the manufacturer, and some mortar must have additive mixed in separately.) Cover the back of the first tile with adhesive, using a ¼" notched trowel.

ALTERNATE: Spread adhesive on a small section of the wall, then set the tiles into the adhesive. Dry-set adhesive sets quickly, so work fast if you choose this installation method.

4 Beginning near the center of the wall, apply the tile to the wall with a slight twisting motion, aligning it exactly with the horizontal and vertical reference lines.

5 Continue installing tiles, working from the center to the sides in a pyramid pattern. Make sure to keep tiles aligned with the reference lines. If tiles are not self-spacing, use plastic spacers inserted in the corner joints to maintain even grout lines (inset). The base row should be the last row of full tiles installed.

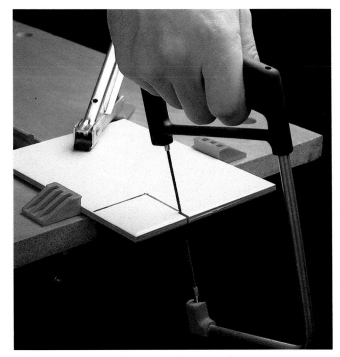

6 Make notches and curved cuts in tile by clamping the tile to a flat surface, then cutting it with a rod saw (a specialty saw with an abrasive blade designed for cutting tile).

7 As small sections of tile are completed, "set" the tile by laying a scrap 2 × 4 wrapped with carpet onto the tile and rapping it lightly with a mallet. This embeds the tile solidly in the adhesive and creates a flat, even surface.

(continued next page)

8 To mark tiles for straight cuts, begin by taping 1/8" spacers against the surfaces below and to the side of the tile. Position a tile directly over the last full tile installed, then place a third tile so the edge butts against the spacers. Trace the edge of the top tile onto the middle tile to mark it for cutting.

9 Cut holes for plumbing stub-outs by marking the outline of the hole on the tile, then drilling around the edges of the outline, using a ceramic tile bit. Gently knock out the waste material with a hammer. Rough edges of hole will be covered by protective plates on fixtures (called escutcheons).

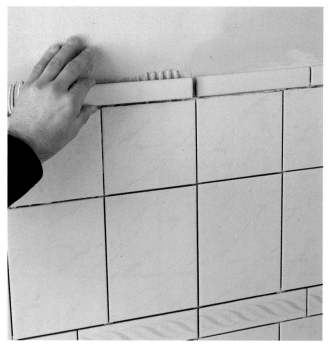

10 Install trim tiles, such as the bullnose edge tiles shown above, at border areas. Wipe away excess mortar along top edge of edge tiles.

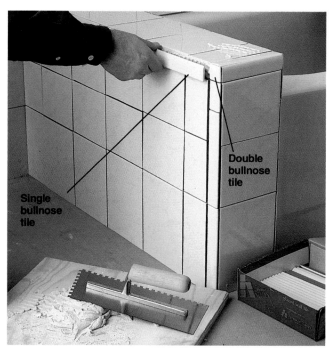

11 Use single bullnose and double bullnose tiles at outside corners to cover the rough edges of the adjoining tiles.

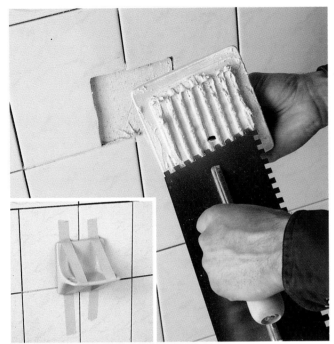

12 Install ceramic accessories by applying dry-set mortar to the back side, then pressing the accessory into place. Use masking tape to hold the accessory in place until the adhesive dries (inset).

13 Let mortar dry completely (12 to 24 hours), then mix a batch of grout containing latex additive. Apply grout with a rubber grout float, using a sweeping motion to force it deep into the joints. Do not grout the joints along the bathtub, floor, and room corners. These expansion joints will be caulked instead.

14 Wipe away excess grout with a damp sponge, then dress the grout lines by drawing a small dowel along all joints.

15 When grout is completely hardened, brush alkaline sealer onto the joints with a small paint brush. Alkaline sealers are better than silicone products for preventing stains and mildew.

16 Seal expansion joints around the bathtub, floor, and room corners with tub & tile caulk. After caulk dries, buff tile with a dry, soft cloth.

Building a Ceramic Tile Countertop

Modern adhesives make it easy for a homeowner to install ceramic tile on a kitchen countertop and backsplash. Because kitchen surfaces are exposed to water, use moisture-resistant adhesive and glazed tiles. Tiles may be sold individually or in mosaic sheets attached to mesh backing. Some tiles have edge lugs that automatically set the width of grout joints. For smooth-edged tiles, use plastic spacers to maintain even grout joints.

A successful tile job requires a solid, flat base and careful planning. Dry-fit the tile job to make sure the finished layout is pleasing to the eye. After installation, seal the tile and grout with a quality silicone sealer to prevent water damage. Clean and reseal the tile periodically to maintain a new appearance.

Everything You Need:

Basic Hand Tools: tape measure, pencil, putty knife, framing square, caulk gun, hammer.

Basic Power Tools: circular saw, cordless screwdriver, orbital sander.

Basic Materials: ceramic tile, ¾" exterior (CDX) plywood, wood strips.

Specialty Tools & Materials: photo, page 90.

Ceramic tiles are available individually, or connected with mesh backing to form mosaic sheets. Ask your dealer to recommend tiles that will stand up to heavy countertop use.

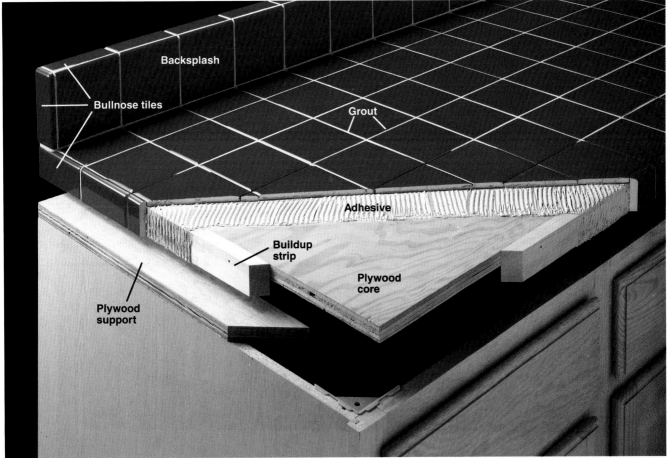

Backsplash

Bullnose tiles

Grout

Adhesive

Buildup strip

Plywood core

Plywood support

Ceramic tile countertop: Countertop core is ¾″ exterior plywood cut to the same size as cabinet. Edges are built up with wood strips attached to outer edges of core. Tiles are set into place with adhesive. Grout fills gaps between tiles. Bullnose tiles, which have rounded edges, are used to cover edges of countertop and backsplash. Backsplash tiles can be installed over a separate plywood core, or directly to wall behind countertop. ¾″ × 3″ plywood supports are attached every 2 feet across base cabinet and around edges of cabinet.

Specialty tools & supplies include: sandpaper (A), denatured alcohol (B), latex grout additive (C), grout (D), silicone caulk (E), silicone sealer (F), carpenter's glue (G), latex underlayment (H), tile adhesive (I), short 2 × 4 wrapped in scrap carpeting (J), tile cutter (K), plastic spacers (L), foam paint brush (M), mallet (N), finish nails (O), wallboard screws (P), tile sander (Q), tile nippers (R), notched trowel (S), grout float (T), scoring tool (U).

How to Build a Ceramic Tile Countertop

1 Cut 3'' wide frame supports from ¾'' exterior plywood. Use 1¼'' wallboard screws or 4d common nails to attach supports every 24'' across cabinet, around perimeter, and next to cutout locations. From ¾'' exterior plywood, cut core to same size as cabinet unit (A × B), using a circular saw.

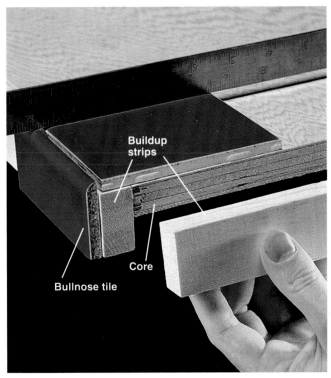

2 If countertop will have bullnose edge tiles, attach 1 × 2 buildup strips of pine or exterior plywood to exposed edges of countertop core, using carpenter's glue and 6d finish nails. Top of strip should be flush with top of core.

Buildup strips

Core

Bullnose tile

Option: for decorative wood edge, attach stained and sealed 1 × 2 hardwood strips to edge of core with carpenter's glue and finish nails. Top of edge strip should be flush with top surface of tile.

3 Position countertop core on cabinets and attach with sheetmetal or wallboard screws driven up through corner brackets inside cabinets. Screws should not be long enough to puncture top surface of core.

4 Use latex underlayment to fill any low spots and cracks in countertop core. Let underlayment dry, then sand smooth.

(continued next page)

5 To create a symmetrical tile layout, measure and mark the middle of the countertop core. Use a framing square to draw a layout line (A), perpendicular to the front edge of the core. Measure along line A from the front edge a distance equal to one full tile, and mark. Use the framing square to draw a second layout line (B) perpendicular to line A.

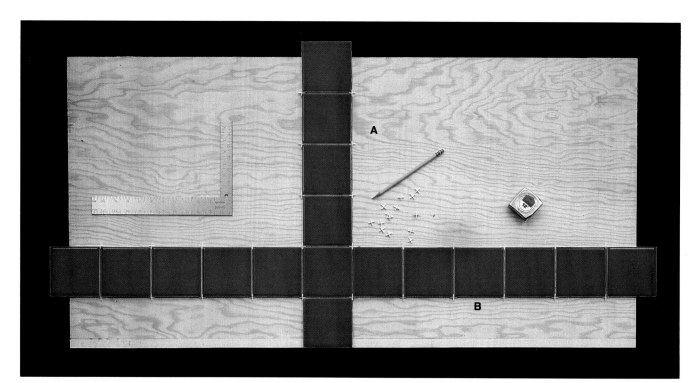

6 Dry-fit rows of tiles along layout lines. Use plastic spacers if tiles do not have self-spacing lugs. If dry-fit shows that layout is not pleasing, line A may be adjusted in either direction. Dry-fit all tiles, and mark cutting lines on any tiles that must be trimmed.

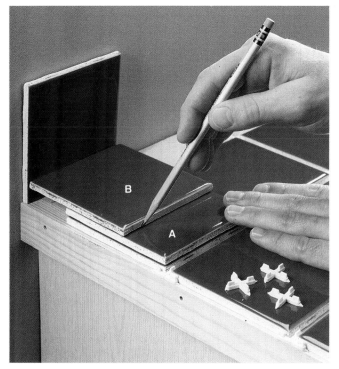

7 Mark border tiles for cutting. To allow for grout, place a tile upright against wall. Place a loose tile (A) over the last full tile. Place another tile (B) against upright tile, over tile A. Mark tile A and cut to fit border space.

8 To make straight cuts, place tile faceup in tile cutter. Adjust tool to proper width, then score a continuous line by pulling the cutting wheel firmly across face of tile.

9 Snap tile along scored line, as directed by tool manufacturer. Smooth the cut edges of tile with a tile sander.

10 For curved cuts, score a crosshatch outline of the cut with tile scoring tool. Use tile nippers to gradually break away small portions of tile until cutout is complete.

(continued next page)

11 Begin installation with edge tiles. Apply a thin layer of adhesive to edge of countertop and back of tile, using a notched trowel. Press tiles into place with a slight twist. Insert plastic spacers between tiles. (Self-spacing tiles require no plastic spacers.)

12 Remove dry-fit tiles next to layout lines. Spread adhesive along layout lines and install perpendicular rows of tiles. Use plastic spacers to maintain even spacing. Check alignment with framing square.

13 Install remaining tiles, working from layout line outward to ends. Work in small areas, about 18" square. Use denatured alcohol to remove any adhesive from face of tiles before it dries. For the backsplash, install a single row of bullnose tiles directly to wall, or build a separate backsplash core from ¾" plywood.

14 After each small area is installed, "set" the tiles. Wrap a short piece of 2 × 4 in scrap carpeting or a towel. Lay block against the tiles and tap lightly with a mallet or hammer. Remove plastic spacers with a toothpick.

15 Mix grout and latex additive. Apply grout with a rubber grout float. Use a sweeping motion to force grout into joints. Wipe away excess grout with a damp sponge. Let grout dry for 1 hour, then wipe away powdery haze. Let grout cure as directed by manufacturer before caulking and sealing.

16 Seal joints around backsplash with silicone caulk. Smooth bead with a wet finger. Wipe away excess caulk. Let caulk dry completely. Apply silicone sealer to countertop with a foam brush. Let dry, then apply second coat. Let dry, and buff with soft cloth.

Edge treatments include rounded bullnose tiles (top) cut to fit edge, and hardwood edge (bottom) shaped with a router. Hardwood edges should be attached and finished before tile is installed. Protect hardwood with masking tape when grouting and sealing the tile job.

INDEX